HOW TO PLAY
the hawaiian
UKULELE
10 EASY LESSONS

HOW TO PLAY
the hawaiian
UKULELE
10 EASY LESSONS

**University of Hawai'i at Manoa
Curriculum Research & Development Group**

Diane Witt & Doris Fuchikami
edited by: Edith Kleinjans & Leon Burton

Mutual Publishing

Library of Congress Catalog Card
Number: 00-109750

Photography by Ray Wong / Pacific Light Studios
Cover Artwork by Peggy Chun
Design by Julie Matsuo

First Printing, September 2000
Second Printing, April 2001
Third Printing, February 2002
Fourth Printing, October 2002
Fifth Printing, July 2003
5 6 7 8 9

ISBN 1-56647- 298-9

Mutual Publishing
1215 Center Street, Suite 210
Honolulu, Hawai'i 96816
Telephone (808) 732-1709
Fax (808) 734-4094
e-mail: mutual@lava.net
www.mutualpublishing.com

Printed in Korea

Appreciation is expressed to the following publishers and copyright owners for granting permission to reprint and/or record their selections. Letters after each citation identify reprint rights (P), recording rights (R), or both (P, R). Every reasonable effort has been made to identify and locate copyright holders of reprint and recording rights for all selections in this book.

"Come Play With Me," melody by Lillian Ito, text by Lois Gordon. Used by permission. (P, R)

"Crazy G," Traditional, arranged by Lillian Ito. Used by permission. (P, R)

"Jazz" by Melvin Maeshiro. Used by permission. (P, R)

"Kau Kau Song, the Island Way," adapted American folk melody, text by Lois Gordon. Used by permission. (P, R)

"Never on Sunday," music by Manos Hadjidakis, lyric by Billy Towne. ©1960 (renewed 1988) EMI UNART CATALOG INC. and LLEE CORP. All rights controlled by EMI UNART CATALOG INC. (Publishing) and WARNER BROS. PUBLICATIONS U.S. INC. (print). All rights reserved. Used by permission. (P)

"Never on Sunday," music by Manos Hadjidakis, lyric by Billy Towne. Used by permission of The Harry Fox Agency, Inc. (R)

"Paniolo Country" by Marcus Schutte, Jr. Used by permission of Mel Leven, Royal Coachman Music Company. (P, R)

"Pretty Paruparō (Pretty Butterfly)," music by Lillian Ito, words by Lois Gordon. Used by permission. (P, R)

"The Sloop 'John B'," Traditional. Copyright ©1975 by Shattinger-International Music Corporation. From 1000 Jumbo, The Magic Songbook, published by Charles Hansen Music and Books, Inc. Used by permission. (P, R)

"Tinga Layo" from Calypso Songs of the West Indies. Copyright of M. Baron Company, Inc. Used by permission. (P, R)

"Yellow Bird" by Alan and Marilyn Bergman and Norman Luboff. ©1957, 1958 (Copyrights Renewed) Threesome Music Co. and Walton Music. All rights reserved. Used by permission. Warner Bros. Publications U.S. Inc., Miami, FL. 33014. (P)

"Yellow Bird" by Alan and Marilyn Bergman and Norman Luboff. Used by permission of The Harry Fox Agency, Inc. (R)

Acknowledgments

The University of Hawai'i expresses kind appreciation to the following people for their generous contributions of time and talent to this project.

Administration

Arthur R. King, Jr., Director
Curriculum Research & Development Group

Donald Young, Associate Director
Curriculum Research & Development Group

Production

Kathy Kakugawa
Katherine Skogmo
Lori Ward

Photographs

Ray Wong, Photographer
Pacific Light Studios

Nani Flores, Model

Contents

Introduction

This book is for anyone who wants to learn to play the ukulele. By working your way through the ten lessons, you will not only develop picking and strumming and fingering skills; you'll also learn to read music and expand your understanding of it.

The lessons include songs, finger exercises, and accompaniments that let you sing along yourself or play along for other singers. The songs display a diversity of styles that will enhance your understanding and widen your appreciation of music. Later you will want to add other kinds of songs to extend your skills and expand your repertoire into areas that intrigue you.

For easy reference, appendices in the back of this book include a glossary, an ukulele chord chart, a fingering chart, and an alphabetical list of performance repertoire included in this book.

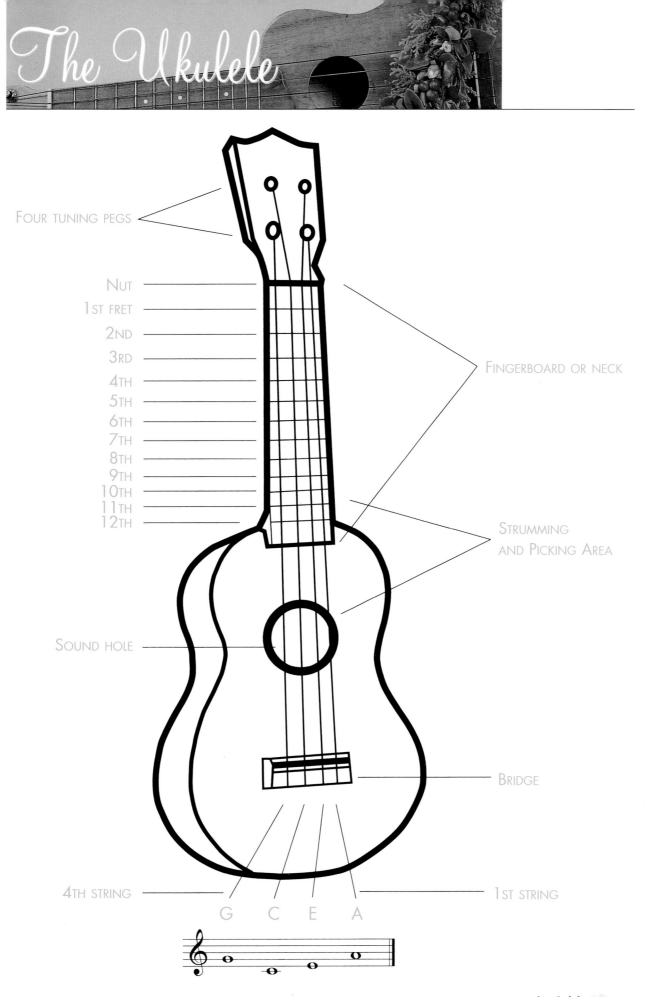

FOUR TUNING PEGS

NUT
1ST FRET
2ND
3RD
4TH
5TH
6TH
7TH
8TH
9TH
10TH
11TH
12TH

FINGERBOARD OR NECK

STRUMMING
AND PICKING AREA

SOUND HOLE

BRIDGE

4TH STRING

1ST STRING

G   C   E   A

In the late eighteenth and early nineteenth centuries, guitars became popular in many parts of Europe. During this period, guitars were created with interesting body designs, some with gut strings, others with wire strings. One guitar used a bow to produce tones; another was struck rather than plucked.

During the expeditions of seafaring peoples, the popularity of guitars spread west to the Americas, south to Africa, and east to Java. Portuguese sailors are credited with introducing a kind of guitar called *cavaco* or *machete* to the Sandwich Islands (Hawai'i) in the 1870s. This instrument—a cross between a guitar and a mandolin—had gut strings. It became known as the ukulele.

In Hawai'i, early ukulele makers using a variety of woods sold instruments for $3 to $5. The ukulele quickly became popular, mostly because it was easy to play and small enough to carry anywhere. Even members of royal families became skillful players. Some people who could not afford to buy ukuleles found ways to make their own, using such unusual materials as coconut shells and cigar boxes. By the late 1900s, the ukulele was the most popular instrument in Hawai'i. In 1980, islanders celebrated what was believed to be the 101st anniversary of the arrival of the ukulele in Hawai'i.

Why is the instrument called ukulele? There are several explanations. According to one attributed to Queen Lili'uokalani, "uku" means gift and "lele" means to come; therefore ukulele was "a gift that came." Perhaps the most intriguing explanation is the most common one—that ukulele means "jumping flea." The word suggests the way performers' nimble fingers jump around the fingerboard.

The ukulele continues to be popular among both young and old in many countries. Its pleasing sounds, its portability, and its relatively low cost qualifies it as an "instrument of the people," offering a way for many to express themselves musically, both singly and in groups.

Tuning the Ukulele Strings

Match the pitch of the four strings to a standard pitch produced by an instrument such as a piano, an organ, or a chromatic pitch pipe.

- Play the pitch G on a standard-pitched instrument.
- Pick the G string and turn the tuning key until the string's pitch matches that of the instrument you are using as a standard.
- Follow the same procedure for the C, E, and A strings.

Holding & Fingering the Ukulele

Hold the ukulele next to your body in an angled position as shown in the photographs. You may change this position slightly when sitting or standing and when picking and strumming.

Sitting position

Standing position

The Left Hand

The left-hand fingers are numbered as follows:

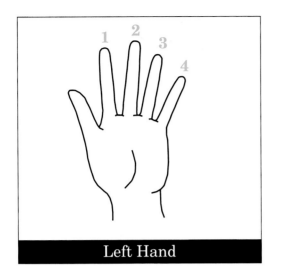

Left Hand

The neck of the ukulele should rest between the thumb and the base of the index finger (1) of your left hand with the strings facing away from you. The space between the fingers lets you bring your left-hand fingers to the proper fingering position. It also keeps the neck of the ukulele from touching your index finger (1).

As you place your left-hand fingers on the strings in the spaces between the frets, hold them in a curved position with the thumb opposite the second finger.

As you shift your hand to higher or lower positions, keep your thumb in position opposite the second finger.

Use the tips of your fingers to press the strings to the fingerboard. Keep your fingernails trimmed. If your nails are long, you will have to flatten your fingers when you play. You will lose finger facility and produce unclear pitches.

The Right Hand

The right hand fingers pick and strum the strings. The following letters are used to identify the fingers. Only these four fingers are used to pick the strings. The little finger remains relaxed and normally moves with the r finger.

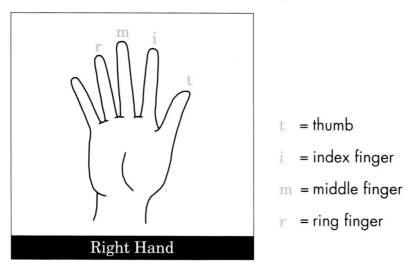

Right Hand

t = thumb

i = index finger

m = middle finger

r = ring finger

Picking & Strumming

Some recommend that beginners learn to pick the strings with the thumb or index finger. For the first lessons, use only the thumb to pick the strings. Lesson 6 introduces the t, i, m, and r fingers for a special kind of picked accompaniment. Depending on what works best for you, use either your thumb or your thumb in combination with other fingers to pick the strings.

The best area of the strings for picking is between the sound hole and the end of the fingerboard. Picking the strings over the fingerboard produces a softer, more mellow sound; picking them over or near the sound hole produces a more twangy sound.

For strumming, as for picking, the best place is between the sound hole and the end of the fingerboard. Strums over the fingerboard will be less brilliant; strums over or close to the sound hole, more brilliant.

Different kinds of strums are introduced in this text. The basic strum in the early lessons requires only the index finger. Later you can use a variety of strums, depending on the sound you want to produce.

Lesson 1

1. Holding the Ukulele

Look at Illustration 1 and learn to hold the ukulele.

2. Picking the Strings

Illustration 2 shows the right-hand thumb position for picking the strings. Notice where the thumb picks the strings, then practice picking the four strings.

Illustration 1

Playing position

Illustration 2

Thumb position

3. Naming the Strings

Look at Illustration 3 and learn the names of the strings. Slowly pick each string eight times, starting with the G string. Sing the names of the strings as you pick them. Try to match the pitch of the strings with your voice as you sing their names.

Illustration 3

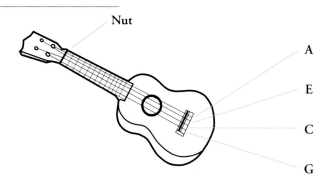

Nut

A

E

C

G

4. Reading a Tablature

Illustration 4 is a tablature showing the four ukulele strings beginning from the **nut** of the instrument. After studying Illustration 4, look again at Illustration 3 to make sure you understand that the tablature represents the first three frets of the fingerboard.

5. Reading Notation for the Strings

Study Example 1 and learn where the pitches of the ukulele strings are notated on the lines and spaces of the music staff. Look at each note and sing the name of the note as you pick each string.

Illustration 4

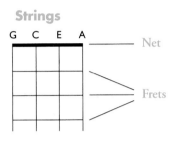

Example 1

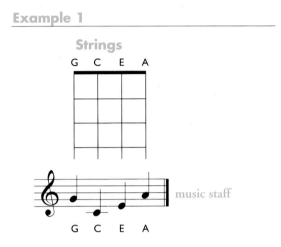

6. Understanding Meter Signatures

Look at Example 2. Notice the $\frac{4}{4}$ meter signature just after the treble clef. The upper 4 shows that there are four beats in each measure. A measure is the distance between barlines. The lower 4 shows that the quarter note (♩) is the "beat note." A double bar (‖) shows the end of a song, and sometimes the end of a section of a song.

Example 2

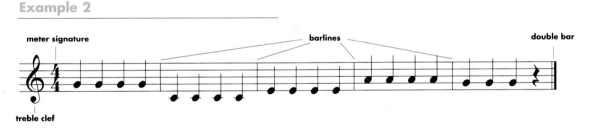

Different kinds of notes show how long a tone should sound. Look at the two kinds of notes in Example 3 and the way they are counted. Notice that a quarter note (♩) lasts one beat, a half note (♩) two beats. A quarter rest (♩) shows one beat of silence.

Example 3

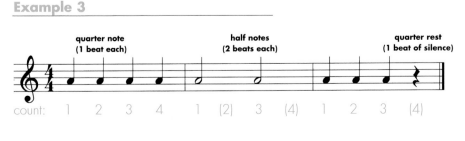

7. Playing Strings from Notation

Learn to play the exercises in Example 4. Count the beats aloud as you play.
Silently count the beats in parentheses. Another option is to sing the names of
the notes while picking the strings.

Example 4

Lesson 2

1. Fingering Strings with the Left Hand

Illustrations 5 and 6 show how the left-hand fingers are numbered and positioned on a string. Place your fingers on the A string as shown. Notice that the tip of each finger is positioned in a space just in back of the fret, the thin metal strip running across the fingerboard. The thumb rests on the back of the neck opposite the second finger.

Illustration 5

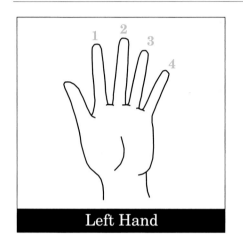

Illustration 6

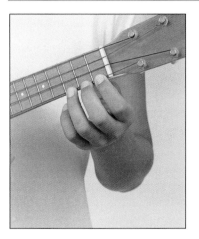

2. Playing the C Chord

Look at Illustration 7 and learn to finger the C chord. Press the tip of your third finger firmly in the third space on the A string. Practice strumming all four strings with your index finger. (See *Picking & Strumming* on page xiv.) Adjust the pressure and position of your third finger on the string so the strings ring freely.

Illustration 7

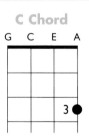

3. Strumming an Accompaniment and Singing

Learn to sing "Row, Row, Row Your Boat." When you know the song, play an accompaniment by strumming the C chord each time you see a slash (/) above a note. Practice until you can strum an accompaniment while singing the melody.

Row, Row, Row Your Boat

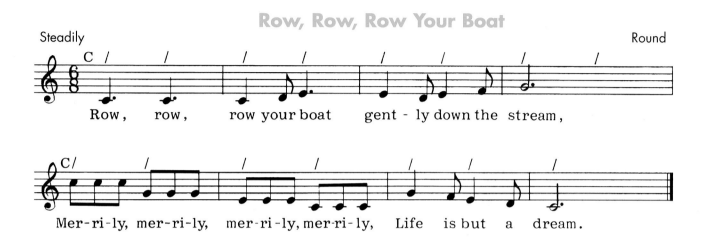

Steadily
Round

Row, row, row your boat gent - ly down the stream,

Mer-ri-ly, mer-ri-ly, mer-ri-ly, mer-ri-ly, Life is but a dream.

4. Playing the F Chord

Look at Illustration 8 and learn to finger the F chord. Practice strumming the chord. Adjust the pressure and position of your left-hand fingers so the strings ring freely.

Illustration 8

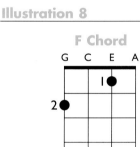

F Chord

G C E A

5. Strumming an Accompaniment and Singing

Learn to sing "Sing Together." When you know the song, play an accompaniment by strumming the F chord each time you see a slash (/) above a note. Practice until you can strum an accompaniment while singing the melody.

Sing Together

England

Sing,   sing to - geth - er,   mer - ri - ly, mer - ri - ly   sing;

Sing,   sing   to - geth - er,   mer - ri - ly, mer - ri - ly   sing;

Sing,   sing,   sing,   sing.

6. Playing the C⁷ Chord

Look at Illustration 9 and learn to finger the C⁷ chord. Practice strumming the chord.

Illustration 9

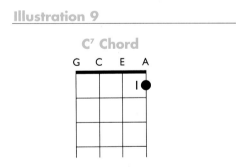

7. Playing a Chord Progression

Review the fingering for the F and C^7 chords; then strum the chord progression in Example 5. The slashes connected by beams (♫) are eighth-note strums. You will need to play two strums to the beat. Practice until you can easily shift between playing the two chords. Keep your left-hand fingers hovering over the fingerboard when not pressing strings, and use as little movement as possible when shifting between the chords.

Example 5

8. Strumming an Accompaniment and Singing

Look at the music of "Polly Wolly Doodle." The letters and slashes above the staff show which chords to strum for an accompaniment. Strum an accompaniment while singing the melody.

Polly Wolly Doodle

Gaily

American Folk Song

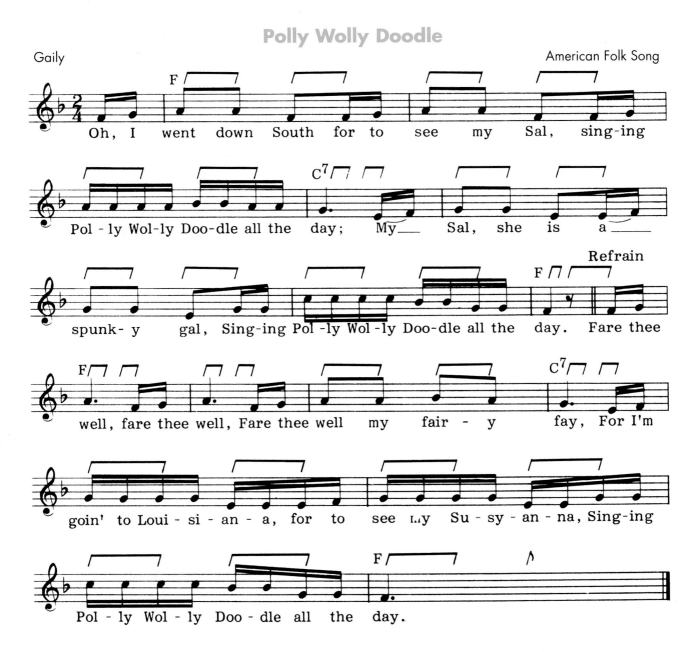

Oh, I went down South for to see my Sal, sing-ing Pol-ly Wol-ly Doo-dle all the day; My__ Sal, she is a__ spunk-y gal, Sing-ing Pol-ly Wol-ly Doo-dle all the day. Fare thee well, fare thee well, Fare thee well my fair-y fay, For I'm goin' to Loui-si-an-a, for to see my Su-sy-an-na, Sing-ing Pol-ly Wol-ly Doo-dle all the day.

2. Oh, my Sal, she is a maiden fair,
      singing Polly Wolly Doodle all the day,
   With curly eyes and laughing hair,
      singing Polly Wolly Doodle all the day.

3. Oh, a grasshopper sittin' on a railroad track,
      singing Polly Wolly Doodle all the day,
   Just pickin' his teeth with a carpet tack,
      singing Polly Wolly Doodle all the day.

4. Behind the barn upon my knees,
      singing Polly Wolly Doodle all the day,
   I thought I heard a chicken sneeze,
      singing Polly Wolly Doodle all the day.

5. He sneezed so hard he couldn't cough,
      singing Polly Wolly Doodle all the day,
   He sneezed his head and tail clear off,
      singing Polly Wolly Doodle all the day.

9. Strumming an Accompaniment and Singing

Learn to sing "Kau Kau Song, the Island Way" using the melody for "Polly Wolly Doodle." When you can sing the melody, strum an accompaniment using the F and C⁷ chords. Let your ears tell you which chords to strum and when to change chords.

Sing the song again, while strumming the chords first with the nail of your index finger, then with your thumb. Compare index-finger strums with thumb strums. Which feels more comfortable? Which produces a better tone? Since both ways are acceptable, choose the way that works best for you.

Kau Kau Song, the Island Way

Words by Lois Gordon   Tune: "Polly Wolly Doodle"

Verse	**Translation**
1. We say, "Hele to my hale for a big luau." That's the Hawaiian way. We say, "Hele to my hale for a big luau." That's the Hawaiian way. Fish and poi, Fish and poi, Fish and poi, lau lau, Fish and poi. We say, "Hele to my hale for a big luau." That's the Hawaiian way.	"Come to my home for a feast."
2. We say, "Moshi-moshi, my friend, tabemashoo." That's the Japanese way. We say, "Moshi-moshi, my friend, tabemashoo." That's the Japanese way. Musubi, musubi, musubi, tofu, musubi. We say, "Moshi-moshi, my friend, tabemashoo." That's the Japanese way.	"Hello. Let's eat together." (Moshi-moshi is the way to say "Hello" on the phone in Japanese)
3. We say, "Yat, nee, sam, see, Noodles when I'm hungry!" That's the Chinese way.	"One, two, three, four"

Verse (Continued)

3. We say, "Yat, nee, sam, see, Noodles when
   I'm hungry!"
   That's the Chinese way.
   Gon lo mein, Gon lo mein, Gon lo mein,
   Chow fun, Gon lo mein.
   We say, "Yat, nee, sam, see, Noodles when
   I'm hungry!"
   That's the Chinese way.

4. We say, "Komosta gayem, Let's eat again."   "Hello, friend."
   That's the Filipino way.
   We say, "Komosta gayem, Let's eat again."
   That's the Filipino way.
   Marunggay, marunggay, marunggay,   "horseradish leaves," "roast pig"
   Lechon Baboy.
   We say, "Komosta gayem, Let's eat again."
   That's the Filipino way.

5. We say, "Usu sau pese," Let's sing a song.
   That's the Samoan way.
   We say, "Usu sau pese," Let's sing a song.
   That's the Samoan way.
   Fala 'ai, fala 'ai, fala 'ai, To pai, fala 'ai.   "pineapple," "dumplings"
   We say, "Usu sau pese," Let's sing a song.
   That's the Samoan way.

6. We say, "Chal mŏ gŏ ssoyŏ," Eat some more-yo!   "The food was very good."
   That's the Korean way!
   We say, "Chal mŏ gŏ ssoyŏ," Eat some more-yo!
   That's the Korean way!
   Kim chee, kim chee, kim chee, Kal bi, kim chee.   "pickled cabbage," "short ribs"
   We say, "Chal mŏ gŏ ssoyŏ," Eat some more-yo!
   That's the Korean way!

7. We say, "Welcome to my home and share some food."
   That's the English (American) way.
   We say, "Welcome to my home and share some food."
   That's the English (American) way.
   Apple pie, apple pie, apple pie, hot dog, apple pie.
   We say, "Welcome to my home and share some food."
   That's the English (American) way.
   Hot dog!

"KAU KAU SONG, THE ISLAND WAY,"
ADAPTED AMERICAN FOLK MELODY, TEXT BY LOIS GORDON. USED BY PERMISSON.

1. Playing the G⁷ Chord

Look at Illustration 10 and learn to play the G⁷ chord. Strum the chord several times, adjusting the position and pressure of your left-hand fingers so all the strings ring freely.

Illustration 10

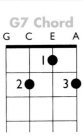

Example 6 is a chord progression using the C and G⁷ chords. Before playing the progression, practice shifting your left-hand fingers between the C and G⁷ chords. When changing from the C chord to the G⁷ chord, slide the third finger back one space and add the first and second fingers. When changing back to the C chord, slide the third finger back up to the third space and lift the first and second fingers. Keep the two unused fingers curved and hovering over the strings, ready to play the G⁷ chord.

Example 6

2. Strumming an Accompaniment and Singing

The *D.C. al Fine* at the end of "Rock-a-My-Soul" means to return to the beginning and repeat the song up to the *Fine* sign. As you play the song, strum an accompaniment to the beat using the C and G⁷ chords. Example 7 shows an introduction that may be strummed before beginning the song.

Example 7

Introduction

Rock-a-My-Soul

Spiritual

Rock - a - my soul,—— in the bos - om of A - bra - ham,

Rock - a - my soul,—— in the bos - om of A - bra - ham,

Rock - a - my soul,—— in the bos - om of A - bra - ham,

Oh, rock - a - my soul. So high you

can't get o - ver it, So low you can't get un - der it,

So wide you can't get round _____ it, You

must go in at the door.

3. Playing a Chord Progression

The chord progression in Example 8 includes the C, F, and G⁷ chords. First practice forming the chords with the left-hand fingers and shifting between them; then strum the progression.

Example 8

4. Strumming an Accompaniment and Singing

Look at the music for "Come Play With Me." Find the chord symbols to learn what chords are included and where the chords change. Strum an accompaniment while singing the song.

Lois Gordon

Come Play With Me

Filipino Song
Lillian Ito

1. Won't you come out and play with me   In the shade of the man-go tree?

Si - pa - si - pa, We'll have some fun   Pick pa - pa - ya when done.

When you come out we'll sing a   song   Hear the birds   as they sing a-long

Hear the ma - ya go, "Ti ri rit   ti ri rit ng i   bon."

2. Won't you come out and play with me
    In the shade of the mango tree?
    "Sipa-sipa," We'll have some fun
    Pick papaya when done
    We'll have fun on a summer day
    Catch a fish in Manila Bay
    See the sun set in western sky
    "Adios," and goodbye.

"Mango" and "papaya" are fruits.
Sipa-sipa is a game of using the feet to keep a shuttlecock from touching the ground.
Maya is a small red bird, the national bird of the Philippines.
Ti ri rit is a bird's trill.
Ng i bon means "Sing together." (*Ng* is pronounced like the *ung* in "sung.")

"COME PLAY WITH ME," MELODY BY LILLIAN ITO, TEXT BY LOIS GORDON.
USED BY PERMISSION.

5. Strumming an Accompaniment and Singing

Strum an accompaniment to "Happiness." When you can strum the accompaniment, try to sing while strumming.

Happiness

1. Playing the Note D

Pick the C string. Then pick the note D by placing your second finger in the space between the first and second frets on the C string.

Example 9

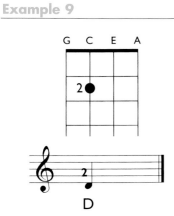

2. Exercises Using the Note D

Example 10 includes exercises that use the note D. Notice the left-hand fingerings above the noteheads (a "0" means that no finger depresses the string), the chord symbols above the staff, and the counting numbers below the notes. Practice the exercises.

Example 10

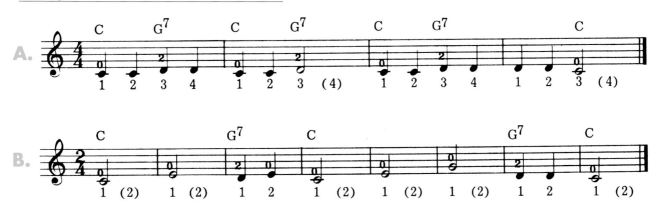

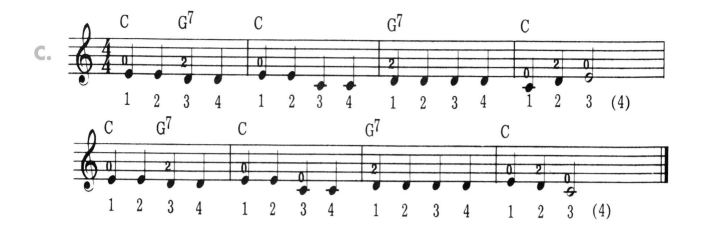

3. Clapping and Counting Aloud, Playing and Singing

Look at the notation for "Jazz." As you learned earlier, a quarter rest ( ) shows silence for one beat. The repeat sign (:|) at the end means to play the selection twice. Practice clapping the rhythm and saying the counting numbers aloud. Count the numbers on rests silently. When you are familiar with the notes and rhythms, learn to pick the melody of "Jazz." You may want to sing the pitch names as you pick the melody.

Jazz

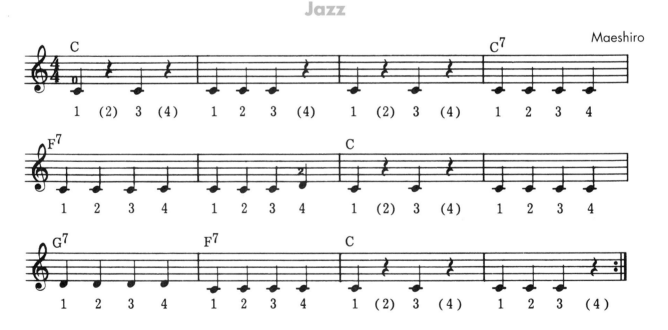

"Jazz" By Melvin Maeshilo. Used by permisson.

4. Counting and Playing Eighth Notes

Eighth notes (♪ ♪ or ♫) receive half a beat and are counted as shown in Example 11. Notice that two eighth notes equal one quarter note (♫ = ♩). Play the C string as quarter notes, then as eighth notes, as shown in Example 11. Count aloud as you play with the beat.

Example 11

Learn to play "Walking" and "Running" with another ukulele player. Then play a duet by picking "Walking" as the other player plays "Running" and vice versa.

5. Playing a Melody

The melody of "Hot Cross Buns" includes eighth, quarter, and half notes. Clap the rhythms and count aloud; then learn to pick the melody.

Hot Cross Buns

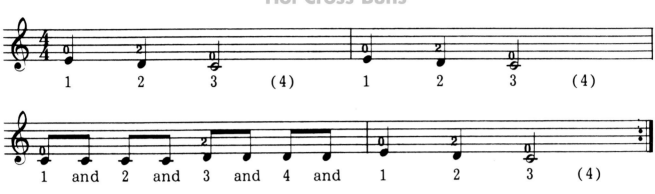

6. Playing a Melody with Chord Strums

Previously you strummed accompaniments and picked melodies as separate parts. The following arrangement of "Hot Cross Buns" combines picking the melody and strumming an accompaniment. Study the music and notice how the picked notes and chord strums are notated and performed. Then learn to play this arrangement by first picking the melody to a steady beat. When you can play the melody, add the C chord strums as indicated by the slashes after the half notes.

Hot Cross Buns

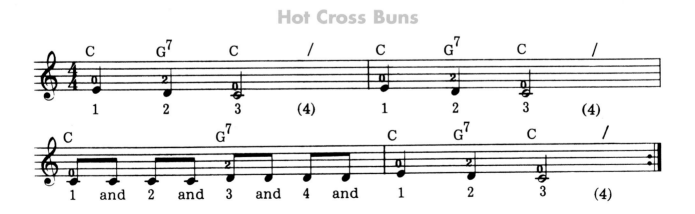

7. Strumming an Accompaniment and Singing

Review the fingerings for the chords used in "C-A-T Popoki Make a Cat." Strum an accompaniment to the song. Then learn to sing the song while strumming an accompaniment. Example 12 shows an introduction that may be played before beginning the song.

Example 12

C-A-T Popoki Make a Cat

Traditional

1. C - A - T po-po-ki make a cat,

R - A - T 'i - o - le make a rat,

M - O - N - K - E - Y ke

ke-ko make a mon-key nō kē - i - a.

2. D-O-G 'ilio make a dog,
   P-I-G pua'a make a pig,
   D-O-N-K-E-Y kekake make a donkey nō kē ia.

3. G-I-R-L kaikamahine,
   B-O-Y keiki kane,
   O-L-D-M-A-N 'elemakule make an old man.

4. Ha 'ina 'ia mai ana ka puana la,
   My country `tis of Hawai'i nei,
   H-A-W-A double I spells Hawai'i.

Lasson 5

1. Picking F and G on the E String

Look at Example 13 and learn to finger the notes F and G on the E string. When you have learned the fingerings, practice picking the exercises in Example 14.

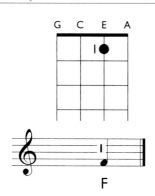

F

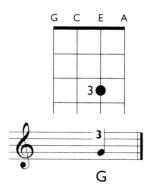

G

Example 14

A.

B.

C.

2. Picking Exercises with Chord Strums

When you can pick the exercises in Example 14, pick them again and strum the accompanying chords indicated by the slash marks.

3. Playing a Duet

Learn to pick the melody of "Gaily the Troubadour." Then learn to pick the harmony part. When you can pick both parts, add chord strums after each half note. The melody and harmony parts are meant to be played together as a duet (a piece for two performers). You can play the duet with a friend by playing the melody the first time, the harmony part the second time, your friend playing the harmony first and then the melody.

Gaily the Troubadour

4. Labeling the Right-Hand Fingers, Playing a Picking Pattern

Example 15 is a picking pattern using the C, E, and A strings. Notice the (a) horizontal lines representing the four strings, (b) letters showing which right-hand finger (thumb or index) picks the strings, (c) eighth notes giving the rhythm for the picking pattern, and (d) letters showing which chords to play.

To begin, finger the F chord with your left hand and pick the strings (C, A, E, A) as eighth notes. The right-hand thumb (t) and index finger (i) alternately pick the strings; (t) picks the C and E strings; (i) picks the A string.

Practice picking this pattern using the F and C⁷ chords.

Example 15

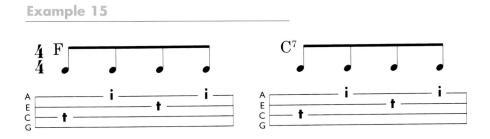

5. Picking an Accompaniment and Singing

When you can play the picking pattern in Example 15, use it as an accompaniment for "Bow Belinda." Practice picking the accompaniment while singing the melody. Create an ending by slowing down the eighth-note picking pattern in the last measure, then playing a slow thumb strum across the four strings after the last note of the melody.

Bow Belinda

Bow, bow, bow Be - lin - da; Bow, bow, bow Be - lin - da;

Bow, bow, bow Be - lin - da, Won't you be my part - ner?

6. Learning to Read and Sing Dotted-Note Rhythms

Study the music for "Oh, Susanna!" Notice that some of the eighth, quarter, and half notes have dots. A dot after a note increases its length by one-half the length of the original note. For instance,

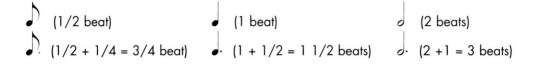

Learn to count these dotted notes.

Oh, Susanna!

Fast

Stephen Foster

the hawaiian ukulele

7. Strumming an Accompaniment and Singing

Strum an accompaniment to "Oh, Susanna!" using the dotted eighth-note and sixteenth-note rhythm (♪. ♬). As shown in Example 16, arrows above notes indicate a down (↓) or up (↑) strum, which you can play using your index finger. Practice strumming until you get the knack of it.

The song has two pick-up notes at the beginning. Start strumming the accompaniment on the downbeat of the first complete measure after the pick-up notes (on the word "come").

Example 16

8. Playing a Melody with Chord Strums

Learn to pick the melody of "Oh, Susanna!" Gradually add the accompanying strums while picking the melody. At first you may want to simplify the strum by playing straight quarter notes, then switch to the dotted rhythms as you gain facility.

Lesson 6

1. Picking B and C on the A String

Look at Example 17 and learn to finger and pick the notes B and C on the A string. Then practice the exercises in Example 18.

Example 17

Example 18

2. Playing the C Scale

The pitches you have learned to pick can be arranged to form the C major scale. Review the notes and fingerings for the scale, then practice it.

Example 19

C Major Scale

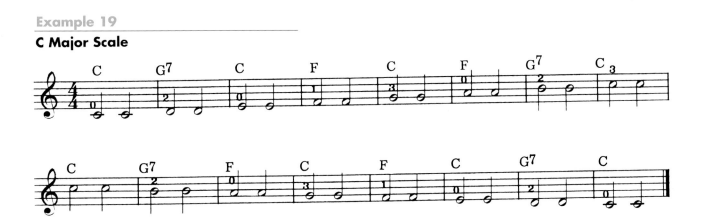

Now learn to play the scale in various rhythms as shown in Example 20. Gradually increase the tempo as you gain facility in fingering and picking the notes. Play these exercises several times as a warm-up when you practice.

Example 20

3. Picking the C Scale and Strumming an Accompaniment

Notice that Example 21 includes the notes of the C scale, with accompanying chord strums indicated by slash marks (/). To play this example,

> a. finger the chord,
> b. pick the scale note on the first beat, and
> c. strum the chord on the second, third, and fourth beats.

G can be played on the open G string or by the third finger on the C string. For this arrangement, the note G will be played as an open string. This fingering will allow you to pick the note G and play the C chord with the third finger.

Example 21

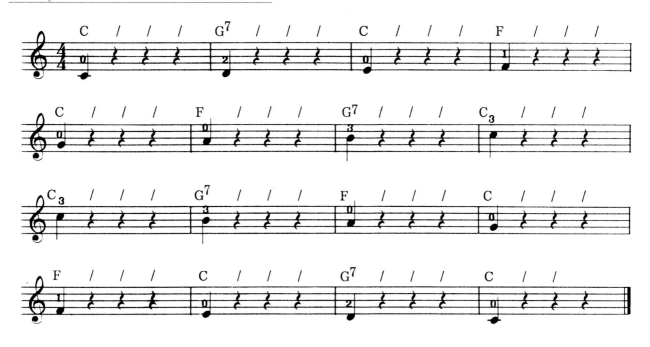

4. Playing a Melody that Includes the C Scale

Learn to pick the melody of "French Folk Song" without the chord strums.
Notice the dotted half-note rhythms that are held for three beats (2 + 1 beats).

French Folk Song

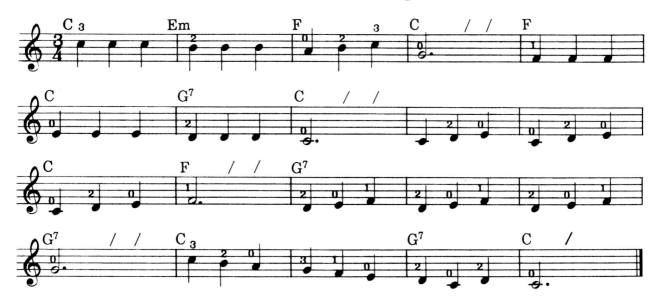

5. Playing a Melody with Chord Strums

Play "French Folk Song" as arranged with chord strums after each dotted half-note. As in Example 21, play the G as an open string so your third finger is available to play the C or G⁷ chord.

6. Playing Tied-Note Rhythms

Look at the music for "On Top of Old Smoky." Notice how some notes are tied together with curved lines, like this: 𝅗𝅥. 𝅗𝅥 and 𝅗𝅥. 𝅗𝅥. 𝅗𝅥. . Ties connect notes of the same pitch, making them sound as one continuous sound.

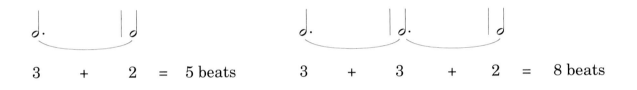

3   +   2   =   5 beats   3   +   3   +   2   =   8 beats

7. Strumming an Accompaniment

Learn to strum an accompaniment to "On Top of Old Smoky." Start with quarter-note strums, then experiment with other rhythms such as these:

Play the first note of each measure a little louder than the rest, as indicated by the accent (>) marks. Emphasizing the first beat of each group of three beats helps to establish the ¾ meter. Remember that the arrows indicate down (↑) and up (↓) strums.

On Top of Old Smoky

8. Playing a Melody with Chord Strums

Learn to pick the melody of "On Top of Old Smoky" with quarter-note strums after the dotted half-notes and tied notes as shown by the slashes above the music. Later you may wish to play "On Top of Old Smoky" using the strums shown in parentheses.

9. Creating an Arrangement of a Song

Learn to pick the melody of "When the Saints Go Marching In." As you play, listen for places where strums may be added. Review other songs such as "On Top of Old Smoky" and "Oh, Susanna!" for ideas. Start by adding strums whenever a tone lasts longer than one beat. Experiment with different strumming patterns until you like your arrangement.

When the Saints Go Marching In

Lively

Spiritual

1. Oh, when the Saints _____ go march-ing in, _____ Oh, when the Saints go march - ing in. _____ Lord, how I want to be in that num-ber, _____ When the Saints go march - ing in.

2. I want to join the heavenly band
   I want to join the heavenly band
   I want to hear the trumpets blowing
   When the Saints go marching in.

3. I want to wear a happy smile
   I want to wear a happy smile
   I want to sing and shout "hallelujah"
   When the Saints go marching in.

4. I want to see those pearly gates
   I want to see those pearly gates
   I want to see those gates standing open
   When the Saints go marching in.

Lesson 7

1. Playing and Singing

Look at the music of "Pretty Paruparō." Notice that this arrangement includes an echo part that can be played by a second player. The melody is notated with stems pointed up; the echo is notated with stems pointed down.

Learn to sing "Pretty Paruparō" (the notes with stems pointing up). If necessary, review the counting for the tied notes:

Strum a simple quarter-note accompaniment as you sing the melody.

Learn to pick the melody of "Pretty Paruparō." Strum chords during the tied notes as an accompaniment. Experiment with various rhythms that fit the style of the song. Play this song as a duet if a second player is available to play the echo notes.

Pretty Paruparō
(Pretty Butterfly)

Lois Gordon

Filipino Song
Lillian Ito

1. 2. But - ter - fly_____   (echo)   In the sky_____ (echo)

Col - ors bright_____ (echo)   Pret - ty Pa - ru - pa -

rō   Dance with me_____ (echo)   Wings so free_____ (echo)

1.   Ma - bu - hay!_____ (echo)   Pa - ru - pa - rong bu - kid.
2.   Wave good - bye_____

(Sing the Coda after the second verse only)

Coda   F   G⁷   C

Pa - ru - pa - rong bu - kid._____

Tagalog

Paruparō (pa-roo-pa-rō), "Butterfly"
Mabuhay (ma-boo-high), "Welcome!"
Paruparong bukid (pa-roo-pa-rong boo-keed), "Field butterfly"

"PRETTY PARUPARŌ (PRETTY BUTTERFLY),"
MUSIC BY LILLIAN ITO, WORDS BY LOIS GORDON. USED BY PERMISSION.

2. Reading a Key Signature

Look at the music for "I Wish I Was Single Again." At the beginning of each staff of music you will see a sharp sign (♯) on the top line representing F. This is a **key signature** indicating that every F in the song is played as F♯.

Learn to finger F♯ on the E string as shown in Example 22. Then learn to pick the melody of "I Wish I Was Single Again." Notice that the dotted half note tied to the half note will be held for five beats (♩.|♩ = 3 beats + 2 beats).

Example 22

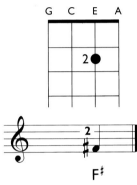

I Wish I Was Single Again

3. Playing the G and D⁷ Chords

Learn to finger the G and D⁷ chords as shown below. Notice that the fingering for the D⁷ chord includes a **bar**. The second finger forms a bar by pressing across all four strings. You must flatten the second finger to play the bar while you curve the third finger to press the string with the tip of the finger.

G Chord

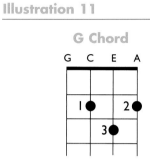

D⁷ Chord

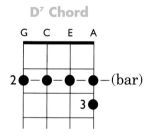

Practice fingering the two chords, plucking the strings one at a time to make sure each string rings freely. When you can finger the chords, practice strumming the following chord progression.

Example 23

4. Strumming an Accompaniment and Singing

Strum an accompaniment to "I Wish I Was Single Again" using the pattern in Example 24. Remember that the arrows indicate down strums (↓) and up strums (↑) with your index finger. The accent (>) indicates a stress on the first beat of each measure to establish the $\frac{3}{4}$ meter.

Example 24

5. Playing a Melody with Chord Strums

Learn to play the melody of "I Wish I Was Single Again" with the chord strums as shown by the slashes. Follow the fingerings shown for the tied notes so you can play the melody notes and strum the accompanying chords.

6. Picking a Melody

Look at the key signature of "Paniolo Country." Notice that every F in the song is played as F♯. Learn to pick the melody.

7. Playing the A⁷ Chord

Learn to finger the A⁷ chord as shown in Illustration 12. Then practice the following progression, which includes the chords from "Paniolo Country." When necessary, use the chord chart in the Appendix to review fingerings for chords.

Illustration 12

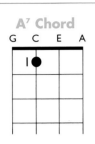

A⁷ Chord

Example 25

$\frac{4}{4}$ G   / / / / | C   / / / / | A⁷   / / / / | D⁷   / / / / | G   / / / / ‖

8. Strumming an Accompaniment and Singing

Sing "Paniolo Country" while strumming an accompaniment using quarter notes.

Paniolo Country

9. Picking an Accompaniment

Practice the following pattern. Then use the pattern to pick an accompaniment to "Paniolo Country."

Example 26

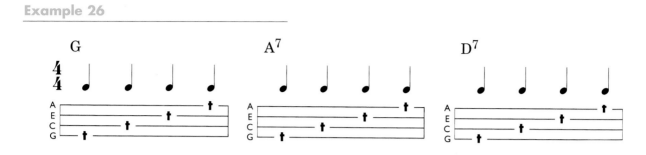

10. Playing a Melody with Syncopated Chord Strums

Learn to play the following strumming pattern. Notice that they do not fall on the normal beats of the measure $\frac{4}{4}$ ♩ ♩|♩ ♩ . The ♪ ♩ ♪ rhythm, called syncopation, disturbs the normal flow of the beats by occurring on the afterbeats at the start of every measure.

Example 27

When you can play the syncopated pattern, study the strums in the music of "Paniolo Country." Learn to pick the melody and strum the chords. You may first pick the melody with simple quarter-note strums, then change to the syncopated rhythms

Lesson 8

1. Strumming an Accompaniment and Singing

Notice that the chords in "Tinga Layo" change every two beats. Strum an accompaniment to the song in eighth notes. Practice until you can strum a simple accompaniment while singing the song.

Tinga Layo

West Indies

Tin-ga Lay - o! Come, lit-tle don-key, come;

Tin-ga Lay - o! Come, lit-tle don-key, come.

1. My don-key walk, my don-key talk, My don-key
2. My don-key eat, my don-key sleep, My don-key

eat with a knife and fork; Tin-ga Lay - o! Come, lit-tle
kick with his two hind feet;

don-key, come; Tin-ga Lay - o! Come, lit-tle don-key, come.

"Tinga Layo" from Calypso Songs of the West Indies.
Copyright of M. Baron Company, Inc. Used by permission.

2. Playing a Melody and Accompaniment that Includes Syncopation

Give special attention to the rhythm in Example 28. This rhythm is an example of syncopation. Learn to clap the rhythm; then listen for where it occurs throughout "Tinga Layo." Notice that this rhythm is similar to the strumming rhythm you played in Lesson 7.

Example 28

3. Strumming a Syncopated Rhythm Pattern

Example 29 is a pattern using the syncopated rhythm from "Tinga Layo." Learn to play the pattern using down (↓) and up (↑) strums as shown. When you have learned the pattern, play it as an accompaniment to "Tinga Layo."

Example 29

etc.

4. Playing a Melody

Learn to pick the melody of "Tinga Layo." Practice until you can play the rhythms included in the song.

5. Picking and Strumming

Look at the strums shown in the music for the half notes in "Tinga Layo." Notice the sixteenth-note slash positioned directly above the half notes. This means that you strum the melody and the accompanying chord at the same time, rather than picking the melody note first then strumming the chords. Since the melody note is sounded as part of the chord, the melody line flows without interruption.

Learn to pick-strum this arrangement of "Tinga Layo," noticing that sometimes the melody notes are picked individually, sometimes strummed within the chords.

6. Reading a Key Signature, Picking a Melody in the Key of F

Look at the key signature for "C-A-T Popoki Make a Cat." Notice that there is a flat sign (♭) on the B at the beginning of each staff. This sign indicates that each B in the song is B♭.

Learn to finger B♭ as shown in Example 30. Then find where B♭ occurs in "C-A-T Popoki Make a Cat." Learn to pick the notes of the song.

Example 30

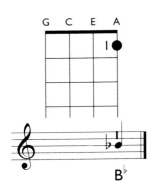

C-A-T Popoki Make a Cat

Traditional

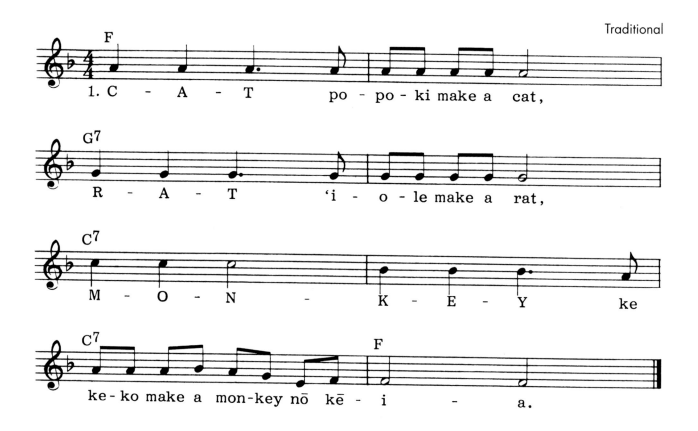

1. C - A - T po-po-ki make a cat,
R - A - T 'i - o - le make a rat,
M - O - N - K - E - Y ke
ke-ko make a mon-key nō kē - i - a.

2. D-O-G 'ilio make a dog,
P-I-G pua'a make a pig,
D-O-N-K-E-Y kekake make a donkey nō kē ia.

3. G-I-R-L kaikamahine,
B-O-Y keiki kane,
O-L-D-M-A-N 'elemakule make an old man.

4. Ha'ina 'ia mai ana ka puana la.
My country `tis of Hawai'i nei,
H-A-W-A double I spells Hawai'i.

7. Strumming an Accompaniment

Strum an accompaniment as you sing "C-A-T Popoki Make a Cat," strum an accompaniment on the beat. Then add the chord pattern shown in Example 31. The chord pattern can be played as an introduction, an interlude between the verses, and a coda at the end of the song.

Example 31

$$\frac{4}{4} \quad \overset{G^7}{/} \; / \; \overset{C^7}{/} \; / \; \Big| \; \overset{F}{/} \; / \; / \; / \; :\Big\|$$

The plan below shows an arrangement of "C-A-T Popoki Make a Cat" with the chord pattern.

Introduction (Chord pattern)
Verse 1
Interlude (Chord pattern)
Verse 2
Interlude (Chord pattern)
Verse 3
Interlude (Chord pattern)
Verse 4
Coda (Chord pattern)

8. Picking a Melody

Look at the key signature for "Lightly Row." Notice that each B in the song is now B♭. Review the fingering for B♭, find where it occurs in "Lightly Row," then learn to play the melody.

Lightly Row

9. Picking and Strumming

Study the strums shown in "Lightly Row." Notice when to pick the melody note followed by a chord strum (slash appears after the note), and when to strum the melody note as part of the strum (slash appears above the note). When strumming the melody note and chord together, the melody note is usually played on the A or E string. At times you will need to adjust the usual chord fingering to include the melody note in the upper strings. The tablature in "Lightly Row" shows suggested fingering for one of these times.

Lesson 9

1. Reading and Playing New Notes

Look at the notes in "Hawaiian Rainbows." Notice the new notes in this song.

- F will become F♯ as shown by the key signature
- The natural sign (♮) next to a note means to play the note without the sharp or flat. For example, the note names and fingerings in measures 2 to 6 would be these:

note: G   F♯   F♮   E   G   A   B♭   B♮   D

- There is a new note (𝄞) to learn to finger.

Hawaiian Rainbows

Modern Hawaiian Song

Ha - wai - ian rain - bows,   White clouds roll   by;

You show your   col - ors   A - gainst the   sky.

Ha - wai - ian rain - bows,   It   seems to   me.

Reach from the   moun - tain   Down to   the   sea.

2. Playing High D Using Extended Fingering, Picking a Melody

Learn to play D on the A string as shown in Example 32. Notice that the first three fingers of your left hand remain in position while the fourth finger extends to finger D in the fifth fret.

Example 32

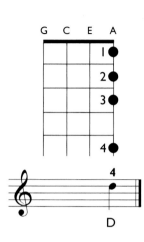

Practice playing D on the A string until you find the fifth fret without looking at the fingerboard. Then learn to pick the melody of "Hawaiian Rainbows."

3. Picking and Strumming

Learn to pick the melody and strum an accompaniment for "Hawaiian Rainbows."

4. Reading and Following the Music

Follow the music as you look at "Red River Valley." Notice that:
- F will become F♯ as shown by the key signature.
- The tied notes will be counted as follows:

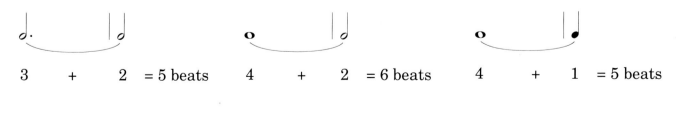

| 3 | + | 2 | = 5 beats | 4 | + | 2 | = 6 beats | 4 | + | 1 | = 5 beats |

- The melody includes high D (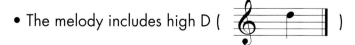)

Red River Valley

Cowboy Song

From this val - ley they say you are go - ing, _____ We will

miss your bright eyes and sweet smile, _____ For they

say you are tak - ing the sun - shine. _____ That has

bright - ened our path - way a - while. _____

5. Playing a Melody with Chord Strums

Learn to pick the melody and strum an accompaniment for "Red River Valley." Notice when to play the melody note and chord together (a slash appears above the note) and how to finger the chord with the melody note (on the tablature above the staff).

Here is a practice plan to learn this and other songs.
a. Learn to pick the melody.
b. Notice where strums will be played as an accompaniment (usually on melody notes that are held for longer duration).
c. Practice playing a simplified arrangement using quarter-note strums.
d. As you gain facility, gradually replace the quarter-note strums with the ones notated in the music.

6. Understanding First and Second Endings

Look at the music of "Never on Sunday." Notice that the last line includes first and second ending repeat signs.

This tells you to play from the beginning to the repeat sign (:‖) at the end of the first ending. Then go back to the repeat sign (:‖) and play again. But the second time through, skip the first ending and play the second ending to the *D.C. al Fine* at the double bar (‖). The *D.C. al Fine* means to go back to the beginning of the piece and play until the *Fine* sign.

Also check the key signature.

Never On Sunday

Manos Hadjidakis & Billy Towne

7. Analyzing a Melody

Read the music to "Never on Sunday" again and notice when parts of the melody are similar to other parts, when they are exactly the same, and when they differ. The first half of the song will be easier to learn if you remember that the lines begin the same way and end with an eighth-note pattern that moves to the note A or F.

8. Learning New Chords, Picking a Melody While Strumming Chords

Be sure you can play all the chords used in "Never on Sunday." If necessary, refer to the Ukulele Chord Chart in the Appendix to learn the fingerings for unfamiliar chords.

Learn to pick the melody with chord strums. Follow the practice plan presented earlier to help you learn this piece.

9. Creating an Arrangement of a Song

Look at the music of "The Sloop 'John B'" and think about how this song might be arranged for the ukulele. Use the following plan to help you create an arrangement for this and other songs. You can begin by learning to play the melody, then adding a simple accompaniment, experimenting with rhythm patterns to create an accompaniment that adds interest and fullness to the melody line. Although the steps move from simple to more difficult, note that more difficult arrangements are not necessarily better. Explore playing this and other selections in various ways. Then decide on one that matches the style and mood of the melody of this song.

a. Learn to pick the melody.

b. Play quarter-note chord strums on melody notes that are held for long durations.

c. Try different strumming patterns that support the style of the melody.

d. Add strums to other melody notes. Experiment and explore strumming patterns that occur on the note or after the note until you find a sound you like.

e. Eventually settle on an arrangement you like that matches the style of the piece.

f. Listen to other performers for interesting strums and rhythms you may use in your playing.

10. Picking and Strumming

After you have created an arrangement of "The Sloop 'John B'," learn to play the one notated here. This arrangement includes syncopated strums, strums that fall after the melody note, and strums that include the melody note. Experiment with including ideas from this arrangement with yours.

The Sloop "John B"

11. Creating Arrangements

Review the songs you learned in earlier lessons. Following the plan outlined in Activity 7, create your own arrangements for the songs using more advanced techniques you have learned.

Lesson 10

This last lesson includes solo selections that you can play at your skill level. Learn each by following the guidelines (see Lesson 9) for practicing new selections and creating arrangements. Start by learning to pick the melody line, then add a simple accompaniment by strumming chords in quarter notes. Experiment with strums and rhythms that match the style of the piece until you create an arrangement you like.

Each time you practice, focus on improving some aspect of your technique. Learning to play the ukulele takes time and focused practice. You make progress not only by learning new songs and playing skills, but also by revisiting and reworking songs you learned earlier. Reviewing lets you apply new skills to familiar material and play with greater facility at a higher performance level.

1. Learn to play the melody of "Yellow Bird"; then create your own arrangement of the song. If you need help, see the strumming suggestions on the music. This arrangement uses a roll or arpeggio indicated by the new symbol (⟨). Follow these procedures to strum a roll on the F chord.

    a. Finger the F chord.
    b. Curl your right-hand fingers into your palm.
    c. Starting with your little finger on the G string, rapidly uncurl
       each finger and strum across the strings with your fingernail.

Practice playing the following chord progression using a roll.

Example 33

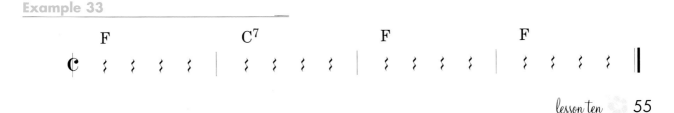

Yellow Bird

Refrain
Rhythmically

Alan and Marilyn Bergman
and Norman Luboff

1. Yel - low Bird, up high in ba-na-na tree.
2. Yel - low Bird, up high in ba-na-na tree.

Yel - low Bird, you sit all a-lone like me.
Yel - low Bird, you sit all a-lone like me.

Did your la - dy frien' leave de nest a-gain? Dat is ver - y sad,
Bet - ter fly a-way, in de sky a-way, Pick - er com - in' soon,

make me feel so bad. You can fly a-way, in the sky a-way,
pick from night to noon. Black and yel - low you, like ba-na - na, too,

Verse

You more luck-y dan me! I al - so have a pret-ty gal.
Dey might pick you some day! Wish dat I was a yel-low bird.

She not with me to - day. Dey all de same de pret-ty gal.
I fly a - way with you. But I am not a yel-low bird.

make dem de nest. den dey fly a - way!
so here I sit. noth - in' else to do!

2. "Crazy G" is a popular piece played with a lot of variations in rhythm, melody, and improvised chords. This arrangement provides a basic plan you can use to develop your own version.

Notice places where you will have to finger the chords and lift your finger to play the melody note, as in measure 5. Practice these fingerings for the chords shown on the tablatures.

When you can play the arrangement of "Crazy G," make up your own version of the piece. Add other chords, a new melody, a new rhythm—whatever seems interesting and satisfying.

3. "Aloha Oe" was written by the last reigning monarch of the Hawaiian Islands, Queen Lili'uokalani. "Aloha Oe," which means "farewell to thee," is a song about parting and the hope of meeting again.

Learn to play the melody of "Aloha Oe"; then create your own arrangement. If you need help, see the suggestions for strums on the music. You will need to play the D⁷ chord using the alternate fingering shown in "Crazy G."

Crazy G

the hawaiian ukulele

"Crazy G," Traditional.
arranged by Lillian Ito. Used by permission.

Aloha Oe
(Farewell to Thee)

With feeling

Queen Liliuokalani

1. Proud-ly glides the rain cloud o'er the cliffs, Blown on-ward by the gen-tle breeze; How the scene re-calls the dis-tant past, And I live once a-gain my mem-o-ries.

Chorus

Fare-well to thee, fare-well to thee, O beau-teous one who lives a-mong the flow-ers, One fond em-brace be-fore I leave, un-til we meet___ a - gain.

2. Thoughts of you will fill the lonely hours,
   I'll see you standing on the shore
   Of this lovely island of my dreams
   Till the day I return to you once more.

1. Haaheo eka ua ina pali Ke nihi ae la i kanahele
   E uhai ana paha i ka liko Pua ahihilehua o uka.
   Aloha oe, aloha oe, E ke ona ona noho i ka lipo;
   One fond embrace a hoi ae au, Until we meet again.

2. O ka halia aloha kai hiki mai Ke hone ae nei i kuu manawa,
   O oe no ka'u ipo aloha A loko e hana nei.
   Aloha oe, aloha oe, E ke ona ona noho i ka lipo;
   One fond embrace a hoi ae au, Until we meet again.

Glossary

Accent (stress)	A musical stress that makes one tone more important than others around it. A dynamic accent is indicated by the sign >.
Accompaniment	Sounds that are meant to enhance a main melody and serve as a background.
Bar	A technique, used in ukulele and guitar performance, of pressing one finger across several strings against the fingerboard.
Barline	A vertical line through the staff that marks off a measure.
Beat	A unit of time, either real or imagined, that controls musical flow.
Chord	Any collection of several pitches sounded together.
Chord progression	Any succession of chords.
Coda	An ending portion of a composition; the part that clearly serves to create a sense of finality.
Composition	A piece of music. The work of a composer.
D.C. al Fine	A symbol on the musical score that means to return to the beginning and repeat the music to the point where the term *Fine* is written.
Duet	Music for two equally prominent parts.
Duration	The length of time consumed by any event, whether a quarter note or an entire musical work.
Echo	To imitate, usually at a softer dynamic level an instant later.
Flat sign (♭)	The notation placed before the head of a note which lowers its pitch one-half tone.
Folk song	Any song whose origins cannot be attributed to a single composer.
Harmony part	A part that sounds simultaneously with a melody and that produces a consonance of sound.
Improvise	To create music spontaneously without fully notated instructions.
Improvised chords	To create spontaneously a chordal accompaniment without notated instructions.
Intonation	Singing or playing "in tune."
Introduction	An introductory section that begins a musical work.
Interlude	Music that connects or "falls between" the main sections of a musical work.
Key signature	Notation at the beginning of a staff that shows which pitches, if any, are to be sharped (♯) or flatted (♭).

Loudness	The strength or intensity of sound in music.
Measure	A group of beats marked off by barlines in music notation.
Melody	Any pattern of successive pitches that projects a sense of contour.
Meter	The measuring or grouping of accented and unaccented beats. The meter of $\frac{3}{4}$, for instance, consists of groupings of pulses in threes.
Meter signature	Vertical numbers at the beginning of a musical work that indicate the number of beats in a measure and which note receives one beat.
Natural sign (♮)	Indicates that after a sharp or flat, the original basic tone is to be restored.
Notation	All of the symbols and signs that make up the writing of music.
Phrasing	The way a phrase of music is performed to combine all tones into a unified statement rather than just a collection of successive tones.
Pick-up notes	Notes of a melody that begin one or two beats before the first complete measure.
Pitch	The high-low aspect of any sound. The keys on the right side of a piano are higher in pitch than the keys on the left side.
Rest	Silence that is precisely prescribed and notated.
Rhythm	The feeling of motion in music arrived at through regularity and diversity of note and rest patterns.
Rhythm pattern	Any succession of sounds that forms a distinctive unit in music.
Roll/Arpeggio (↯)	The successive sounding of the notes of a chord. On the ukulele, a roll is a technique to play an arpeggio using the fingernails to strum across the strings.
Scale	Any ordering of successive pitches within an octave—usually to represent the pitch content of a musical work.
Sharp sing (♯)	The notation placed before the head of a note raises its pitch one-half tone.
Staff	The five lines on which musical notation is placed to indicate pitch.
Syncopation	A rhythm pattern that at some point does not correspond to normal metric flow; the displacement of an accent pattern.
Tablature	A system of notation used mostly for stringed instruments. On the ukulele, a tablature shows where to place the left hand to finger notes and chords.
Tempo	The rate of flow of a musical passage; its speed through time.
Text	The words that make up a song.
Tied notes	A slightly curved line showing that two notes of the same pitch are to be performed as one continuous sound.
Tone	Any sound that lasts long enough to project a pitch and timbre.
Tremolo	A rapid strumming of the strings with the index finger for the duration of the note.
Tuning	The act of adjusting the pitches of an instrument to a standard pitch.
Verse	Sections of a song sung to different lines of text.

Ukulele Chord Chart

A

A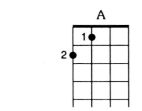
A⁷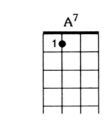
Am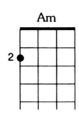
Am⁷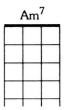

A♯ /B♭

 A♯/B♭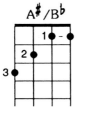
A♯⁷/B♭⁷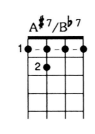
A♯m/B♭m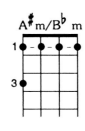
A♯m⁷/B♭m⁷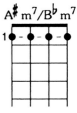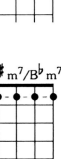

B

 B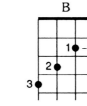
B⁷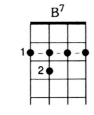
Bm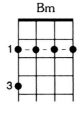
Bm⁷

C

C
C⁷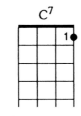
Cm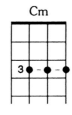
Cm⁷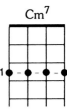

C♯ /D♭

C♯/D♭
C♯⁷/D♭⁷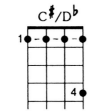
C♯m/D♭m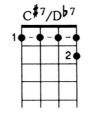
C♯m⁷/D♭m⁷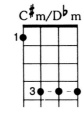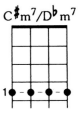

D

D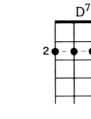
D⁷
Dm
Dm⁷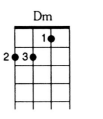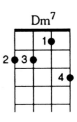

D# / E♭

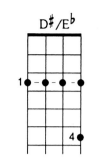
D#/E♭

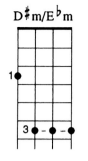
D#7/E♭7

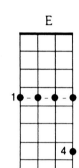
D#m/E♭m

D#m7/E♭m7

E

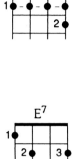
E

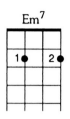
E7

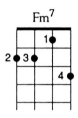
Em

Em7

F

F

F7

Fm

Fm7

F# /G♭

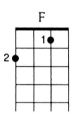
F#/G♭

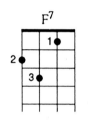
F#7/G♭7

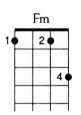
F#m/G♭m

F#m7/G♭m7

G

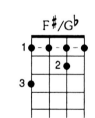
G

G7

Gm

Gm7

G# /A♭

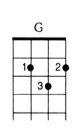
G#/A♭

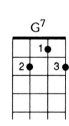
G#7/A♭7

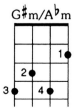
G#m/A♭m

G#m7/A♭m7

64 the hawaiian ukulele

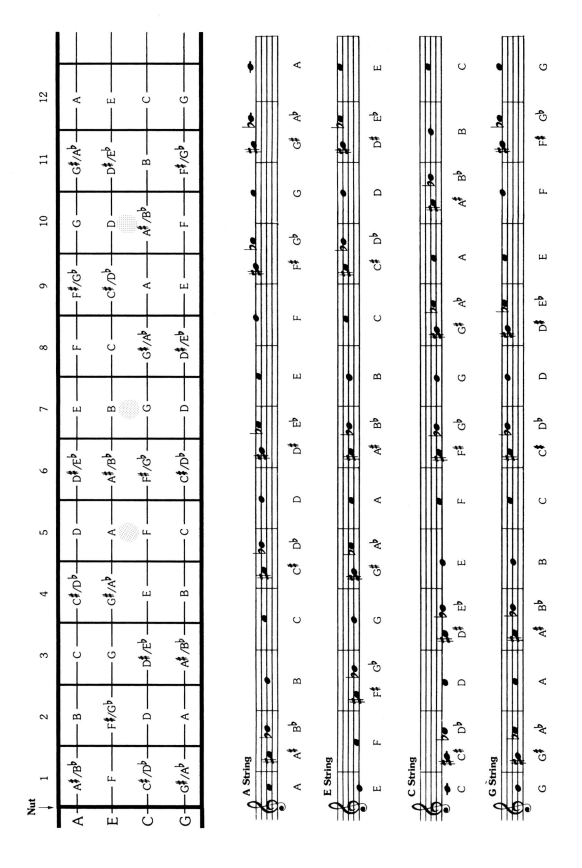

Alphabetical List of Performance Repertoire